Word Therapy

McDougal & Associates

Servants of Christ and Stewards of the
Mysteries of God

Word
Therapy

Putting the Word of God
To Work in Your Life

by

Rev. Dr. Omolara Idowu

Word Therapy
Copyright © 2021—Omalara Idowu
ALL RIGHTS RESERVED UNDER U.S., PAN-
AMERICAN AND INTERNATIONAL COPYRIGHT
CONVENTIONS
No part of this publication may be reproduced,
stored in a retrieval system or transmitted in any form
by mechanical, electronic, photocopying, recording or
otherwise without the prior written consent of the author.

Unless otherwise noted, all Scripture references are from the
King James Version of the Bible, public domain. References
marked NLT are from *The Holy Bible, New Living Translation*,
copyright © 1996, 2004, 2007 by Tyndale House Foundation.
Used by permission of Tyndale House Publishers, Inc., Carol
Stream, Illinois. Used by permission. All rights reserved.

Published by:

McDougal & Associates
18896 Greenwell Springs Road
Greenwell Springs, LA 70739
www.thepublishedword.com

McDougal & Associates is an organization dedicated to
spreading the Gospel of the Lord Jesus Christ to as many
people as possible in the shortest time possible.

ISBN: 978-1-950398-45-4
eBook 978-1-950398-46-1

Printed in the U.S., the U.K. and Australia
For Worldwide Distribution

Dedication

This book is dedicated to believers who know their rights in the Kingdom of God and act on them.

Contents

Foreword by Bishop Abiola Idowu 9

Introduction.................................... 13

1. No More Bondage 17

   WORD THERAPY....................................... 27

2. Releasing Abundant Power for Living.... 31

   WORD THERAPY....................................... 37

3. Born to Be Successful 39

   WORD THERAPY....................................... 45

4. Living a Fortified Life 47

   WORD THERAPY....................................... 57

5. Walking in the Power of Liberty 59

   WORD THERAPY....................................... 68

   Author Contact Page 70

THE RAIN AND SNOW COME
DOWN FROM THE HEAVENS
AND STAY ON THE GROUND
TO WATER THE EARTH.
THEY CAUSE THE GRAIN TO GROW,
PRODUCING SEED
FOR THE FARMER
AND BREAD FOR THE HUNGRY.
IT IS THE SAME WITH MY WORD.
I SEND IT OUT, AND IT AL-
WAYS PRODUCES FRUIT.
IT WILL ACCOMPLISH
ALL I WANT IT TO,
AND IT WILL PROSPER EV-
ERYWHERE I SEND IT.
ISAIAH 55:10-11, NLT

The ministry of the Word is the force behind every victory, salvation, prosperity and wholeness in life because it is based on covenants. The Bible says, in Psalm 89:34:

My covenant will I not break, nor alter the thing that is gone out of my lips.

The Word is sprinkled by the blood, ascertaining the efficacy and the authority that backs the Scriptures (see Hebrews 9:18-19). Therefore, the Word of God is a force that brings God into the scene anytime that Word is believed. The major challenge is that the Word has been trivialized and watered down as opinion and concepts by culture and tradition, including religious inclinations, and people have lost the power in the Word of God by not believing it and acting on it.

The Word is a Person. He is a mighty force that holds the Universe together:

> *In the beginning was the Word, and the Word was with God, and the Word was God. All things were made by him; and without him was not any thing made that was made.* John 1:1 and 3

God is the Word, He made all things by the Word He spoke, and John 1:14 says that the Word is Jesus Christ. When you speak the Word, you are applying Jesus Christ to the situation directly. Whatever cannot stand in the way of Jesus Christ cannot stand in the way of His Word.

Dr. Omolara Idowu has opened our eyes to the therapeutic nature the Word of God has when we put that Word into operation by speaking it out in faith. It handles everything we may be going through in life. As the Bible says, God *"upholds all things by the Word of his power"* (Hebrews 1:3).

> *Who being the brightness of his glory, and the express image of his person, and upholding all things by the word of his power, when he had by himself purged our sins, sat down on the right hand of the Majesty on high.*

It's time to take charge and rule the Universe and live the life of Heaven on Earth by practicing the Word of God. God can be trusted because He will keep what He has promised. Take the Word as your medication, as described by the Scriptures, and you will live in dominion.

God bless you!
Shalom!
Bishop Abiola Idowu

Introduction

The Shunammite woman of 2 Kings 4 is a great example of those who believe in the blessing of God in spite of their circumstances. She had waited a long time before her child was finally born, and everything went smoothly for a while. But then, a few short years afterward, she faced a situation that could have entirely derailed her faith and caused her to go astray. Her son was in the field one day with his father when he was suddenly and mysteriously taken ill. He was rushed home to the care of his mother, but there was little she could do for him. Within a few hours, he was dead.

Had this woman not known how to operate by faith in God and His blessing, she might have reacted like any other mother—screaming, "My baby is dead! Why has this happened to me? Where is God?" Instead, without saying a single negative word, this woman headed off immediately to meet the prophet of God.

When her husband asked her where she was going, her answer was, *"It shall be well!"* (verse 23). When she met the prophet, he asked her if everything was well with her, and she replied, *"It is well"* (verse 26). At that moment, her circumstances didn't look blessed at all, but she believed that she *was* blessed, so like our father, Abraham, she called *"those things that be not as though they were":*

> *(As it is written, I have made thee [Abraham] a father of many nations,) before him whom he believed, even God, who quickeneth the dead, and calleth those things which be not as though they were.* Romans 4:17

This dear lady was holding on to the Word of God. She was griping the blessing by faith and would not let it go, despite the contrary circumstances. The result was that the prophet went there and prayed for the child, and he came back to life.

But what do you think opened the door for Elisha to bring that boy back to life? Was it because he was a prophet? No! It was the faith of the mother in her God and in His promises. She believed in the word of her prophet and the Word of her God. Her faith agreed with the Word of God and raised her son from death. That's what faith does. It practices *Word Therapy.*

This precious woman gave us a perfect picture of how faith in the blessings of God responds in a time of crisis. Faith opens its mouth and confesses the Word of God about every situation. Faith says, *"It is well!"*

You cannot fight thoughts with thoughts. It won't work. You can only fight thoughts with the Word of God. Luke 21:15 tells us:

> *For I will give you a mouth and wisdom, which all your adversaries shall not be able to gainsay nor resist.*

Also remember this promise:

> *Thou shalt also decree a thing, and it shall be established unto thee: and the light shall shine upon thy ways.* Job 22:28

Negative thoughts have no defense against faith-filled words. Your words are so powerful that, according to Jesus Himself, you will be either justified by them or condemned by them:

> *For by thy words thou shalt be justified, and by thy words thou shalt be condemned.*
> Matthew 12:37

Your words are so important that you will be called upon to give an account of them on the Day of Judgment:

That's how serious words are to God. You are blessed, and you are highly favored. Come with me now as we explore some more *Word Therapy.*

Shalom!
Pastor Omolara Idowu

Chapter One

No More Bondage

And God said, Let us make man in our image, after our likeness: and LET THEM HAVE DOMINION over the fish of the sea, and over the fowl of the air, and over the cattle, and over all the earth, and over every creeping thing that creepeth upon the earth. Genesis 1:26

Freedom is the proof of love, and God's will for you is total freedom. Freedom means living without hindrances or domination, the ability to put everything in its proper place, having complete liberty in every part of your life.

God hates bondage, and He never intended for man to live in bondage. God Himself does no want to dominate you. He gave you the power of free will. Nothing is designed to rule over you here on this Earth. God's perfect will for every man, woman, boy and girl on the face of the earth is freedom.

Many want freedom, but they are too lazy to seek it or to live in it once they have found it. If you are desperate to be free, get desperately enough to seek the truth. Jesus said:

> *And ye shall know the truth, and the truth shall make you free.* John 8:32

You shall know what? You shall know *the truth*. And knowing *the truth* will enable you to live without hindrances and restraint. This is the way man was created to live. God created you to rule, not to be ruled.

True freedom, however, is a function of the truth. Because many are too lazy to seek the truth, they become victims of ignorance and live in bondage. Our salvation experience is just the gateway into a wonderful life of freedom and blessing in Christ.

So, if freedom comes through the discovery of truth, we must seek the truth. Let us start with the question: What is truth?

The answer to this important question is this: Truth is a Person, and that Person is Jesus Christ. Knowing Jesus is knowing freedom. Knowing that He is for you is knowing freedom. Understanding what He has said about you will make you free. He Himself declared:

> *I am the way, the truth, and the life: no man cometh unto the Father, but by me.*
>
> John 14:6

Jesus is the Truth. He says to you today, "Knowing Me means that you are free."

The disciple known as Simon Peter struggled with this issue. His name, Simon, meant Unstable, and he was unstable before he met Jesus. When Jesus confronted Peter on the Sea of Galilee one day and challenged him to launch his nets to catch fish, he answered, *"We have toiled all the night, and have taken nothing"* (Luke 5:5). Things were not going well for this man called Simon Peter. There is nothing more frustrating in life than exerting effort and having no results. That can discourage the strongest of individuals.

But there was something else at work in the heart of Simon Peter that day. He seemed to be, for the moment at least, a failure at his profession, and he and his family would surely suffer economically because of it. But he had met Jesus, and He felt that Jesus had some sort of power that he didn't yet understand.

Jesus was different from other men. Peter sensed something very special about this man and His words. This must have been what caused him to have second thoughts that day. His situation looked dismal, but if Jesus said for him to cast his net again, there must be a reason. When Jesus spoke, things happened, good things. Therefore, the answer of Peter was this:

We have toiled all the night, and have taken

nothing: nevertheless at thy word I will let down the net.

Peter was an experienced fisherman, and he knew the fish were simply not running that day. BUT he was willing to take a chance on Jesus. Jesus' words made things happen. What happened next was amazing to everyone, especially to Peter:

And when they had this done, they inclosed a great multitude of fishes: and their net brake. And they beckoned unto their partners, which were in the other ship, that they should come and help them. And they came, and filled both the ships, so that they began to sink. When Simon Peter saw it, he fell down at Jesus' knees, saying, Depart from me; for I am a sinful man, O Lord. For he was astonished, and all that were with him, at the draught of the fishes which they had taken. Luke 5:6-9

God's Word changed Peter's life, and it will change your life too. The one thing that can change your life is for you to make Jesus the final say in everything you say and do. He always knows best, and His Word never fails.

You need to understand: God is not playing games with your life. He has something wonderful in mind for you, and the knowledge of that good thing can be discovered in His Word:

> *That the God of our Lord Jesus Christ, the Father of glory, may give unto you the spirit of wisdom and revelation in the knowledge of him.* Ephesians 1:17

God didn't save you, only to have you pulled down by the people around you who want to spit on you. Just for you, God has prepared the riches of His glory, and He has put everything under the feet of Jesus. Therefore, if you have made Jesus Lord of your life, you too are an overcomer in all things.

Jesus is our Head, and we are His Body:

> *Now ye are the body of Christ, and members in particular.* 1 Corinthians 12:27

We are to be fully engaged in His work to bless the people of this world. Too many have been deceived and still consider themselves to be little more than dust. But the man who fell (Adam) did not look like me. He came from the dust, but I did not. When I got saved, I was now from Christ, not from dust:

> *For we are his workmanship, created in Christ Jesus unto good works, which God hath before ordained that we should walk in them.* Ephesians 2:10

I am created in Christ, not in dust.

The apostle Paul knew that this revelation was not from a man:

> *But I certify you, brethren, that the gospel which was preached of me is not after man.* Galatians 1:11

This is from God, and He has declared that I am a new creature in Christ:

> *Therefore if any man be in Christ, he is a new*

creature: old things are passed away; behold, all things are become new. 2 Corinthians 5:17

Not only are you a brand new being; you are created *"in the likeness of His resurrection"*:

For if we have been planted together in the likeness of his death, we shall be also in the likeness of his resurrection. Romans 6:5

Just three days after Jesus had died, Mary Magdalene, who knew Him very well, saw Him, but she could no longer recognize Him. And that is what happens to you when you get saved. You are so changed that people can barely recognize you. Everything about you has changed. You have been reborn in Christ.

"Adam," the Bible shows us, *"was not deceived"*:

And Adam was not deceived, but the woman being deceived was in the transgression.
1 Timothy 2:14

No matter the situation, don't run away from God; run toward Him. You resemble the last Adam, which is our Lord Jesus. Don't put yourself down by believing that you are not qualified for this freedom. Just read the Parables of the Lost Sheep, the Lost Coin, and the Lost Son, all in Luke 15. Our God specializes in things that were once lost. You are now born of Christ and have become a new creation in Him.

The source of freedom is not just a prayer; it's the truth, and Jesus is the Truth. Jesus is saying to anyone who is lost today, "If you can just return home, you will be free." Do not allow anyone to bring you under condemnation. You are a child or God.

There, in Luke 5, when Peter said to Jesus, *"Depart from me, for I am a sinful man,"* that was before he knew the Truth. That's what we all need—the Truth.

If a church is giving you money but not giving you truth, leave that place. Make God your Source, and He will supply your every need. Your commitment to the Truth will determine your freedom in life.

Every one of us will have to one day stand before God and give an account of our lives and how we have lived them here on Earth. Therefore, make a big deal out of God's presence. Be committed to Him and to His Word. I know the old excuse: "I don't have enough time," but we each have 168 hours in every week. Make time for God. Make time for His Word. Your future depends on it. Your destiny depends on it.

In Luke 15:22–23, the Word of the Lord says, concerning the Prodigal Son, that his father gave him new clothes, which signified beauty; gave him his own ring, which signified authority; and gave him new shoes, which signified dominion. Stop seeing yourself as weak and insignificant, and start seeing the Christ in you today.

Now, let us start the therapy. Make the following declarations from the Word of God:

1. I AM THE RIGHTEOUSNESS OF GOD IN CHRIST JESUS, AND I HAVE PUT ON MY GARMENT OF RIGHTEOUSNESS. THEREFORE, LET NO ONE TROUBLE ME, FOR IN MY BODY THERE IS A MARK THAT SHOWS THAT I BELONG TO JESUS.

> *From henceforth let no man trouble me: for I bear in my body the marks of the Lord Jesus.* Galatians 6:17

2. THERE WILL BE NO MORE BONDAGE IN MY LIFE, FOR I HAVE BEEN REDEEMED.

> *If the Son therefore shall make you free, ye shall be free indeed.* John 8:36

HE HAS CALLED ME TO FREEDOM, SO I SHALL LIVE FREE.

3. I HAVE THE HOLY SPIRIT IN ME, AND THEREFORE I AM FREE:

Now the Lord is that Spirit: and where the Spirit of the Lord is, there is liberty.
2 Corinthians 3:17

I AM FREE.

4. THE TRUTH IS THAT I AM FREE:

And ye shall know the truth, and the truth shall make you free. John 8:32

5. BY HIM, EVERYONE WHO BELIEVES IS FREED FROM EVERY EVIL THING. EVERY CHALLENGE OF LIFE FACING ME NOW IS GONE. I AM FREE FROM EVERY EVIL:

And by him all that believe are justified from all things, from which ye could not be justified by the law of Moses. Acts 13:39

6. I [PUT YOUR NAME HERE] HAVE
   BEEN EMPOWERED TO BECOME A
   SON/DAUGHTER OF GOD, WITH ALL
   OF ITS PRIVILEGES.

> *But as many as received him, to them gave*
> *he power to become the sons of God, even to*
> *them that believe on his name.*   John 1:12

Beloved, I want you to declare these words over your life every day. And don't forget to share your testimonies. Send your emails to Lirrypop980@gmail.com.

Chapter Two

Releasing Abundant Power for Living

But as many as received him, to them gave he power to become the sons of God, even to them that believe on his name.   John 1:12

Because you are a citizen of the Kingdom of God, power is part of your package for living, and when you are walking in power, everything must submit to you.

Say unto God, How terrible art thou in thy works! through the greatness of thy power shall thine enemies submit themselves unto thee.   Psalm 66:3

Yes, you now have power over sickness, disease and afflictions. And you cannot carry power and not carry authority. When you speak, everything must obey. Nothing and no one on this earth can resist you. Everything that has been resisting you must bow.

Jesus Christ had this testimony. The Heaven opened over Him, and there was a voice that spoke:

> *This is my beloved Son, in whom I am well pleased.* Matthew 3:17

In this way, Jesus was given authority and dominion. He could be in charge because He was God's Son. And because He was God's Son, everything and every one would bow to Him and obey Him. And you and I are heirs of Christ:

> *And if children, then heirs; heirs of God, and joint-heirs with Christ; if so be that we suffer with him, that we may be also glorified together.* Romans 8:17 KJV

If Jesus had a special place with the Father, then you have that same place. If you are a citizen of God's Kingdom, then you have the same authority as the twenty-four elders of the book of Revelation. I have a witness in my spirit that, from today, you will be taking over, and you will do it in the name of Jesus.

You are a product of heavenly power, so it's time for you to rise up and silence the mockers. You may still live in a human body, but you have a touch of Heaven on your soul. You have a reborn spirit that gives you the authority to speak the things of Heaven, things here on Earth and even things under the Earth.

You have power to walk like Jesus did on the Earth, and everything is made subject to you because you are in charge. God wants you to operate in the same realm as He operates. Jesus said:

Believest thou not that I am in the Father, and the Father in me? the words that I speak unto you I speak not of myself: but the Father that dwelleth in me, he doeth the works. John 14:10

Like Him, I can speak with boldness and authority because of what the Father has said:

Verily, verily, I say unto you, He that believeth on me, the works that I do shall he do also; and greater works than these shall he do; because I go unto my Father.
John 14:10

Jesus is with the Father right now, so you have the power and authority He left to His followers. The devil knows very well that you have this power, but he still lies and tells you that you somehow have to pay for it. This is the philosophy of men, and we must beware of it:

Beware lest any man spoil you through philosophy and vain deceit, after the tradition of men, after the rudiments of the world, and not after Christ. Colossians 2:8

As human beings, we often look to people of experience as being wise and having correct conclusions. The truth is that a great many are blinded to the truth.

> *In whom the god of this world hath blinded the minds of them which believe not, lest the light of the glorious gospel of Christ, who is the image of God, should shine unto them.*
> 2 Corinthians 4:4

All those who have not yet seen the light of the glorious Gospel of Christ are blinded to truth. Cling to Christ, who is Truth. Cling to His Word that never fails, and you will be wiser than your generations.

Now, as *Word Therapy*, say this with your mouth, and mean it with your heart:

I AM A CHILD OF GOD!
I HAVE THE POWER RIGHT NOW.
AMEN!

The devil wants to play a blame game. "You have not prayed enough." "You have not fasted enough." Don't let the enemy bring any other philosophy to you other than the pure truth of God's Word.

In Mark 16:18, Jesus said *"They shall take up serpents."* Everything in this passage is based on who believers are in Christ. The essence of this teaching is for us to speak the way Jesus spoke and act the way He acted:

> *And these signs shall follow them that believe; In my name shall they cast out devils; they shall speak with new tongues; they shall take up serpents; and if they drink any deadly thing, it shall not hurt them; they shall lay hands on the sick, and they shall recover.* Mark 16:17-18

Defraud ye not one the other, except it be with consent for a time, that ye may give yourselves to fasting and prayer; and come together again, that Satan tempt you not for your incontinency.   1 Corinthians 7:5

Avoid the philosophies of men that can destroy the efficacy of the Word of God.

Now, do this *Word Therapy*:

GOD LOVES ME!
I AM ACCEPTED WITH THE BELOVED!
THERE IS NOTHING SATAN CAN DO
  ABOUT MY CASE BECAUSE JESUS
  PAID MY PRICE!

What shall we say then? Shall we continue in sin, that grace may abound? God forbid. How shall we, that are dead to sin, live any longer therein? Know ye not, that so many of us as were baptized into Jesus Christ were baptized into his death? Therefore we are buried with him by baptism into death: that like as Christ was raised up from the dead by the glory of the Father, even so we also should walk in newness of life. For if we have been planted together in the likeness of his death, we shall be also in the likeness of his resurrection: knowing this, that our old man is crucified with him, that the body of sin might be destroyed, that henceforth we should not serve sin. Romans 6:1-6

Beloved, depend upon God's grace rather than believing in your own efforts. He is able.

As before, I want you to declare these words over your life every day. And don't forget to share your testimonies. Send your emails to Lirrypop980@gmail.com.

Chapter Three

Born to Be Successful

And God blessed them, and God said unto them, Be fruitful, and multiply, and replenish the earth, and subdue it: and have dominion over the fish of the sea, and over the fowl of the air, and over every living thing that moveth upon the earth.

Genesis 1:28

Everything came with a purpose and intention, and you were born for success. But every one of us must read the manual, and that is the Word of God. Yes, I said: READ THE MANUAL.

The Manual says that you are redeemed to be blessed. God raised Jesus up to bless you and me:

> *Unto you first God, having raised up his Son Jesus, sent him to bless you, in turning away every one of you from his iniquities.*
>
> Acts 3:26

You were born to be the salt of the earth and the light of the world:

> *Ye are the salt of the earth: but if the salt have lost his savour, wherewith shall it be salted? it is thenceforth good for nothing, but to be cast out, and to be trodden under foot of men. Ye are the light of the world. A city that is set on an hill cannot be hid.*
>
> Matthew 5:13-14

You were ordained for life in Christ Jesus:

> *This letter is from Paul, chosen by the will of God to be an apostle of Christ Jesus. I have been sent out to tell others about the life he*

has promised through faith in Christ Jesus.
2 Timothy 1:1, NLT

If you want to want to enjoy everything that God has planned for to make you successful, here are some biblical secrets:

1. Seek First God's Kingdom

Seek the Kingdom of God above all else, and live righteously, and he will give you everything you need. Matthew 6:33, NLT

If you know you are the responsibility of the King, you will pay Him more attention, and because of that, you will escape every detention and avoid every destruction. Seek Him first! You are a member of His Kingdom, and He cares about you!

Each time you seek the Kingdom first, you have committed yourself to every breakthrough, every success, and every promotion. The Word of the Lord has said, *"He will give you everything you need." Everything* means every thing. There are no Kingdom giants who have any other foundation. This is it. Let it be the foundation of your success too. Stand strong and tall on the promise of God.

2. Never Entertain Discouragement

To be discourage is to make God small. The only thing that will last forever is His Word:

> For ever, O LORD, thy word is settled in heaven. Psalm 119:89

The Word of God is eternal, unchanging, fixed, and established. God has already commanded your blessing. He is just waiting for you to declare it:

> Who is he that saith, and it cometh to pass, when the LORD commandeth it not?
> Lamentations 3:37

> Remember the former things of old: for I am God, and there is none else; I am God,

and there is none like me, declaring the end from the beginning, and from ancient times the things that are not yet done, saying, My counsel shall stand, and I will do all my pleasure. Isaiah 46:10

That's is our God! Worship Him!

And all that dwell upon the earth shall worship him, whose names are not written in the book of life of the Lamb slain from the foundation of the world. Revelation 13:8

3. Use What You Have and Refuse to Think You Are Helpless.

One of the most terrible things we can do is to look down on what God esteems. The cost determines the value, and I have been purchased by the blood of Jesus:

Forasmuch as ye know that ye were not redeemed with corruptible things, as silver and gold, from your vain conversation received by tradition from your fathers; but

> *with the precious blood of Christ, as of a lamb without blemish and without spot.*
>
> 1 Peter 1:19

God has given me a mouth and wisdom that none of my adversary will be able to gainsay nor resist (see Luke 21:15).

Your mouth is an asset. Use it and declare your breakthrough, your success, and your progress in life:

> *Christ hath redeemed us from the curse of the law, being made a curse for us: for it is written, Cursed is every one that hangeth on a tree: that the blessing of Abraham might come on the Gentiles through Jesus Christ; that we might receive the promise of the Spirit through faith.* Galatians 3:13–14

4. Organize Yourself

Planing is proof that you know that God is involved in your life. God doesn't plan for us. Planing is the responsibility of man, not God

God changed Abram's name to Abraham, as recorded in Genesis 17:5, and he left and started telling people about his change of names. God confirm it, and Abraham was successful *"in all things"*:

> *And Abraham was old, and well stricken in age: and the* Lord *had blessed Abraham in all things.* Genesis 24:1

You, too, are blessed. Declare it with your mouth. What God has said will never return to Him void:

> *So shall my word be that goeth forth out of my mouth: it shall not return unto me void, but it shall accomplish that which I please, and it shall prosper in the thing whereto I sent it.* Isaiah 55:11

If the Lord has declared it, then you can declare it too. He has declared that you don't have to be sick. Declare it:

I SHALL NOT BE SICK!

I SHALL NOT BE HURT!
I SHALL NOT BE POOR!

Jesus said:

> *For verily I say unto you, That whosoever shall say unto this mountain, Be thou removed, and be thou cast into the sea; and shall not doubt in his heart, but shall believe that those things which he saith shall come to pass; he shall have whatsoever he saith.* Mark 11:23

YES, I WILL HAVE WHATEVER I SAY!
I RECEIVE IT IN THE NAME OF JESUS!
THE LORD SUPPLIES ALL MY NEEDS
    ACCORDING TO HIS RICHES IN
    GLORY!
MY HEAVENS ARE OPEN!
MY RAIN IS FALLING ... IN THE NAME
    OF JESUS!

Beloved, again, I want you to declare these words over your life every day. And don't forget to share your testimonies. Send your emails to Lirrypop980@gmail.com.

Chapter Four

Living a Fortified Life

*Praise ye the LORD. Sing unto the LORD a
new song, and his praise in the congregation
of saints. Let Israel rejoice in him that made
him: let the children of Zion be joyful in
their King. Let them praise his name in the
dance: let them sing praises unto him with
the timbrel and harp. For the LORD taketh
pleasure in his people: he will beautify the
meek with salvation.* Psalm 149:1-4

Yes, our Lord takes pleasure in His people
and He beautifies the meek with salvation.
You cannot know Him and not be grateful.
He is worthy to be praised.

That is why we praise His name in the dance. When we give Him Thanks, He responds with beauty.

To be beautiful is to be admired, to excel. Every advancement in life is a product of a voice from Heaven. That powerful voice makes you invincible and unconquerable and puts your adversary on the run. The voice of the Lord puts pressure on anything and everything. The voice of the Lord is powerful:

> *The voice of the LORD is upon the waters: the God of glory thundereth: the LORD is upon many waters. The voice of the LORD is powerful; the voice of the LORD is full of majesty. The voice of the LORD breaketh the cedars; yea, the LORD breaketh the cedars of Lebanon.* Psalm 29:3-5

Why is God's voice so powerful? Because it comes from Him, a most powerful Person. He spoke to Adam and Eve in the Garden of Eden, and it brought them fear because they had sinned against Him:

And they heard the voice of the Lord God walking in the garden in the cool of the day: and Adam and his wife hid themselves from the presence of the Lord God amongst the trees of the garden. Genesis 3:8

When the voice of the Lord comes to you, your wilderness will change to a city. The voice of the Lord delivered the children of Israel from danger at the Red Sea:

And the Lord said unto Moses, Wherefore criest thou unto me? speak unto the children of Israel, that they go forward.
Exodus 14:15

And He will deliver you too.

There was no time for tears or sorrow. God said, "Tell the children of Israel to go forward," and when they obeyed, they walked across the sea on dry ground.

The voice of the Lord will give you a miracle too. The thing in your life that looks like a Red Sea will leave you alone today.

Remember what happened to Peter:

And Simon answering said unto him, Master, we have toiled all the night, and have taken nothing: nevertheless at thy word I will let down the net.   Luke 5:5

He was toiling and struggling ... until the voice of the Lord came to him. Then he was changed. As we have seen, at first it was, *"We have toiled all night and caught nothing."* Life didn't seem fair just then. Things were not going well. But, after the voice of the Lord came, it was, *"At thy word."* And it worked for Peter and his companions.

Please don't analyze the Word of God with human intelligence. Just accept it for what it is, believe it, and act on it. When you do, your life will be changed. Your bad circumstances will be swept away:

He sent his word, and healed them, and delivered them from their destructions.
                                                    Psalm 107:20

The Word of the Lord is God's tool to get things done. We have never seen God physically at any time, but we have seen His Word, and His Word is who He is. He upholds all things by the Word of His power:

> *God, who at sundry times and in divers manners spake in time past unto the fathers by the prophets, hath in these last days spoken unto us by his Son, whom he hath appointed heir of all things, by whom also he made the worlds; who being the brightness of his glory, and the express image of his person, and upholding all things by the word of his power, when he had by himself purged our sins, sat down on the right hand of the Majesty on high.*
>
> Hebrews 1:1-3

The sun, the moon, and the stars cannot resist or hinder the Word of God. There is victory in that Word.

What kinds of words do you need to speak to ensure your victory? Job declared:

> *How forcible are right words! but what doth your arguing reprove?* Job 6:25

Right words are what? They are FORC-IBLE! One right word that comes to you can change your story forever. Isaiah said:

> *Ye shall have a song, as in the night when a holy solemnity is kept; and gladness of heart, as when one goeth with a pipe to come into the mountain of the LORD, to the mighty One of Israel. And the LORD shall cause his glorious voice to be heard, and shall shew the lighting down of his arm, with the indignation of his anger, and with the flame of a devouring fire, with scattering, and tempest, and hailstones. For through the voice of the LORD shall the Assyrian be beaten down, which smote with a rod.* Isaiah 30:29-31

God comes to us with a song, and you and I have a mouth to sing. So, Sing! As you are singing that song, you will hear the glorious voice of the Lord.

Elisha understood the power of a song:

> *And Elisha said, As the LORD of hosts liveth,*
> *before whom I stand, surely, were it not that*
> *I regard the presence of Jehoshaphat the king*
> *of Judah, I would not look toward thee, nor*
> *see thee. But now bring me a minstrel. And*
> *it came to pass, when the minstrel played,*
> *that the hand of the LORD came upon him*
> 2 Kings 3:14-15

In that moment of crisis, they needed a voice and a song for that voice to sing. You no longer need tears. Speak what the Lord says, and your victory will also come.

God is ready to do greater and greater things for us:

> *And this is but a light thing in the sight of*
> *the LORD: he will deliver the Moabites also*
> *into your hand.*   2 Kings 3:18

So many miracles come to us through worship, through singing and declaring what God has said.

On this particular occasion, three kings were in a wilderness place where there was no water. But they realized that what God was saying about their situation, His living Word, had the power to change things. Therefore, they acted upon that Word, and it did just what God said it would do. God's Word is His tool to change every life story, and that includes your story:

> In the beginning was the Word, and the Word was with God, and the Word was God. The same was in the beginning with God. All things were made by him; and without him was not any thing made that was made. John 1:1-3

Look again at verse 1:

> In the beginning was the Word, and the Word was with God, and the Word was God.

The Word is a Person. Thank God for what He has done, His acts, the manifestations of

His power. Thank God for His love for each of us. He has not destined us to shame.

Ten lepers came to worship Jesus, and when they did, the voice of the Lord began to work in their situation. But don't wait until you can see it. Act on it, and the seeing will come. God's Word will never fail. It will produce a harvest in your life.

The Word of the Lord—His divine direction, instruction or correction—can come to us in many ways: through the Bible, through prophecy, through dreams and visions, through preaching and teaching or even at the hands of angels.

The Word of God is alive and is right there with you. Release your faith into what He has said to you:

> *And, behold, there came a leper and worshipped him, saying, Lord, if thou wilt, thou canst make me clean. And Jesus put forth his hand, and touched him, saying, I will; be thou clean. And immediately his leprosy was cleansed.* Matthew 8:2-3

Jesus said it, and what He said then happened. Please don't joke around with worship. There is a voice that always comes with worship. Get serious with God and when He speaks, you will have His Word to depend on.

God has structured your life so that everything contrary to His Word must bow before you. Through Him and His Word, we have power over all evil:

> *Forasmuch then as the children are partakers of flesh and blood, he also himself likewise took part of the same; that through death he might destroy him that had the power of death, that is, the devil.*
>
> Hebrews 2:14

Jesus suffered so that we would not have to suffer:

> *And the God of peace shall bruise Satan under your feet shortly. The grace of our Lord Jesus Christ be with you. Amen.*
>
> Romans 16:20

Now, as *Word Therapy*, say this with a loud voice:

SATAN, GO BACK TO WHERE YOU BE-
    LONG!
YOU ARE UNDER MY FEET!
YOU ARE NOT IN MY WALLET!
YOU ARE NOT IN MY BODY!
YOU ARE NOT IN MY HEAD!
YOU ARE UNDER MY FEET!

> *For when he spoke, the world began! It ap-
> peared at his command.* Psalm 33:9, NLT

AMEN!

Don't forget, Beloved, I want you to declare these words over your life every day.
Also don't forget to share your testimonies.
Send your emails to Lirrypop980@gmail.
com.

Chapter 5

Walking in the Power of Liberty

For the sin of this one man, Adam, caused death to rule over many. But even greater is God's wonderful grace and his gift of righteousness, for all who receive it will live in triumph over sin and death through this one man, Jesus Christ. Romans 5:17, NLT

God will not do anything without first telling you. There is no empty destiny. There is no failure in the Kingdom. We are all destined to reign in life as kings through the redemption that Christ purchased for us on the cross of Calvary.

This has nothing to do with where you are from or who you are. It has every thing to do with Jesus Christ, and that is what God is looking for. It satisfies Him.

Because of the obedience of Christ, not our own obedience, we can reign in life. His gift of righteousness empowers us to do what we could not do on our own.

God is not using any one of us for an experiment. He is not taking us through something just so that He can change our story. No, God is a good teacher. He has experienced everything Himself before He even began writing the sacred Scriptures, and everything that He has done is good:

> *Then God looked over all he had made, and he saw that it was very good!*
>
> Genesis 1:31, NLT

It was not just acceptable or good. It was *"very good."* God proved it before He re-leased it. Then He made provision for our redemption: He would Himself die for the whole world, not just a few. He did not die just for those who are in the Church. He died for all mankind everywhere:

> *For this is how God loved the world: He gave his one and only Son, so that everyone who believes in him will not perish but have eternal life.* John 3:16, NLT

For who? For *"everyone."*
God has even given us His glory:

> *And having chosen them, he called them to come to him. And having called them, he gave them right standing with himself. And having given them right standing, he gave them his glory.* Romans 8:30, NLT

Everything needed to make you great is all around you, but it's in the dark. You just need to turn on the light. You can be looking for something in the dark, but if there is no light, even though it is right there before you, too often you cannot see it. The moment you turn the light on, you will see it. It was not the light that manufactured it; the light just revealed it. You just need to turn the light on.

You have passed by many things and not taken advantage of them because you didn't see them well enough. Everything that redemption offers belongs to you. If you can just get enough light to let you see what you have, you can quickly locate the money you need and the peace and joy you have been lacking. It has all been provided for. You just need to see it and receive it.

God's Word brings us the needed light:

> *The teaching of your word gives light,*
> *so even the simple can understand.*
> Psalm 119:30, NLT

There is only one thing that can terminate your progress and hinder everything you attempt to accomplish in this world, and that is darkness. God's Word shatters darkness. You have everything packaged in you to make you as extraordinary as you were destined to be. Only darkness can hinder your destiny.

God's Spirit in you enables you:

> *The Spirit of God, who raised Jesus from the dead, lives in you. And just as God raised Christ Jesus from the dead, he will give life to your mortal bodies by this same Spirit living within you.*   Romans 8:11, NLT

Joel prophesied:

> *"Then, after doing all those things,*
> *I will pour out my Spirit upon all people.*
> *Your sons and daughters will prophesy.*
> *Your old men will dream dreams,*
> *and your young men will see visions."*
> Joel 2:28, NLT

This was the same Spirit that moved upon the void and caused all things to be created. God said He would pour this same Spirit out upon us. We don't necessarily need to feel it; we just need to acknowledge it and receive it.

Acts 2 records the coming of the Spirit into the world on the Day of Pentecost. As with

Creation, when the Spirit came, it changed everything. Every emptiness, every void was filled. And each time the Spirit of the Lord manifests today, something new is created.

Everything that changed the life of Abraham is available to you. There was a covenant that God made with Abraham that exempted him from the evil influence all around him.

What is a covenant? A covenant is a divine agreement between God and man. It is based upon an oath and established by the shedding of blood. Because blood is involved , life is involved.

When it is our covenant-keeping God who is committed to us in covenant, that covenant is as strong as God is strong. It is irrevocable, and it causes God to do things that are very uncommon. If, for instance, a man is wrong, if he is in covenant with God, God will not allow anyone else to rebuke the man. He must deal with the wrong Himself.

Because of the strength of our covenant with God, He has said:

I will not violate my covenant
or alter what my lips have uttered.
Psalm 89:34, NLT

"I will not," God said. And He won't.
Receive His gift of righteousness:

(For if by one man's offence death reigned
by one; much more they which receive
abundance of grace and of the gift of righ-
teousness shall reign in life by one, Jesus
Christ.) Therefore as by the offence of one
judgment came upon all men to condemna-
tion; even so by the righteousness of one the
free gift came upon all men unto justifica-
tion of life. Romans 5:17-18, KJV

It is our covenant with God that puts everything in place so that His blessings can
flow to us without any hinderance. His covenant is stronger than any force of darkness,
and it slaps the devil in the face.

God understands better than anyone the
forces of darkness that rule this world, but
He has exempted us.

After man fell in the garden of Eden, it was God's desire to restore everything back to him. He found a man called Abraham and cut a covenant with him. This covenant had nothing to do with Abraham's prayer. The grace of God located him, and through Abraham, God entered into this earth to restore the garden of Eden back to us. Then He added some new things on top of that.

When God cut a covenant with this man, it not only changed his story and made him a star. He said to Abraham, "Although you are a stranger here, this land is yours." And He didn't even consult the landowner (see Genesis 17:4-10):

> *God gave the promises to Abraham and his child. And notice that the Scripture doesn't say "to his children," as if it meant many descendants. Rather, it says "to his child" — and that, of course, means Christ.*
>
> Galatians 3:16, NLT

The blessing was given to Abraham and, through him, transferred to the seed, which is Christ. Jesus then came here to carry the blessings to *His* seed, which means to you and to me.

Jesus declared:

> *All that belongs to the Father is mine; this is why I said, "The Spirit will tell you whatever he receives from me."*
>
> John 16:15, NLT

> *The Father loves his Son and has put everything into his hands.*   John 3:35, NLT

Paul wrote to the Roman believers:

> *And since we are his children, we are his heirs. In fact, together with Christ we are heirs of God's glory. But if we are to share his glory, we must also share his suffering.*
>
> Romans 8:17, NLT

The seed by covenant came with the blessing. If you are a child of God, all things are yours as a joint heir.

Therefore, as *Word Therapy*, say this out loud:

EVERYTHING THAT GOD GAVE TO
  JESUS BELONGS TO ME TOO.

Paul wrote to the Colossian believers:

> *I, Paul, have been sent on special assignment by Christ as part of God's master plan. Together with my friend Timothy, I greet the Christians and stalwart followers of Christ who live in Colosse. MAY EVERYTHING GOOD FROM GOD OUR FATHER BE YOURS!*
>
> Colossians 1:1-2, MSG

EVERY GOOD THING COMES FROM
  GOD AND COMES TO ME. I BELIEVE
  IT, AND I RECEIVE IT!

I AM IN COVENANT WITH ALMIGHTY
  GOD. THEREFOR, DEVIL, TAKE
  YOUR HANDS OFF OF MY BUSI-
  NESS. WHATEVER IS HOLDING ME

BOUND, YOU ARE CUT OFF NOW
IN THE NAME OF JESUS. ANYTHING
THAT WOULD TRY TO DEFEAT ME IS
DESTROYED. FOR I AM A CHILD OF
THE LIVING GOD.

AMEN!

Don't forget, Beloved, I want you to declare these words over your life every day. Also don't forget to share your testimonies. Send your emails to Lirrypop980@gmail.com. And may God bless you as you practice *Word Therapy*.

Author Contact Page

You may contact Rev. Dr. Omolara Idowu in the following ways:

eMail: lirrypop980@gmail.com

Phone: 904-469-5724